Manners Matter

LIVING THE GOLDEN RULE
FOR KIDS OF ALL AGES

HERMINE HARTLEY
ILLUSTRATED BY AL HARTLEY

PROMISE PRESS
An Imprint of Barbour Publishing

Manners Matter

LIVING THE GOLDEN RULE
FOR KIDS OF ALL AGES

© 2002 by Hermine Hartley

ISBN 1-58660-723-5

Cover image © GettyOne, Inc.

Interior illustrations by Al Hartley.

Published by Promise Press, an imprint of Barbour Publishing, Inc., P.O. Box 719, Uhrichsville, Ohio 44683, www.promisepress.com

 Member of the
Evangelical Christian
Publishers Association

Printed in the United States of America.

5 4 3 2 1

To my family,
for without living the
Golden Rule each day
with each other,
we would never be the
close, loving family
that we are.

contents

introduction

This is a revised edition of *The Family Book of Manners*, which was written predominantly for children.

For some time, there has been a real need for a manners book for "kids" of all ages. Many of today's adults have grown up eating in front of the TV or on lap trays with TV dinners or in fast-food restaurants. When they are invited to a dinner in someone's home, a business dinner, or an upscale restaurant, there may be confusion or embarrassment as to which fork to use or which glass belongs to them.

In this disposable society it appears that manners have been as disposable as fast-food plates. We are polluting with much of our trash, and it seems as though we are polluting our society with foul language and crude behavior, as well.

A recent national survey stated that 79 percent of the 2013 adults surveyed in January 2002 by the research group Public Agenda said a lack of respect and courtesy in American society is a serious problem. Many people feel awkward and insecure in meeting people or introducing them to others in a social setting.

This book is easy to read and written for the average person. It covers essential basics to help you feel good about yourself.

Sadly, morals, manners, and spiritual values have declined and the Golden Rule (Luke 6:31) "Do to others as you would have them do to you," which is part of every major world religion, expresses the key to manners and the key to how we should act in life in every situation.

Manners are more than using the right fork—they're using the right attitude. Our behavior affects our relationships.

This book shows that manners are not stuffy rules wearing white tie and tails, but they show up in shorts and jeans, as well. Good manners show respect and consideration for others.

This updated edition is the result of my being spurred on by numerous newspaper articles with titles such as: "Self-esteem Promoted to Combat Social Ills," "Bad Habits Are Improved by Improving Personal Images," "Are Morals Outmoded," "Don't Be a Dinner Table Dunce," and "Large Companies Hiring Manners Teachers to Aid Executives."

It's the height of hypocrisy to expect our children to have better manners than those we demonstrate in our own lives.

Society has changed significantly since the first book

was written. We live with more high-tech conveniences than ever before, so we have included manners for using a vast array of electronic devices, including wireless phones and the Internet. We've expanded some sections as well as added sections on business manners, dating, tipping, customer service. . .and more.

Without getting too complicated this is really a contemporary "manners catch-up."

THE *Golden* RULE

So whatever you wish that men would do to you, do so to them.

—Christianity

It's interesting to note that the world's major religions all have their own versions of the GOLDEN RULE:

That which is hateful to you, do not to your fellow man.

—Judaism

One precept to be acted upon throughout one's whole life. . . Do not unto others what you would not have them do to you.

—Confucianism

Do not hurt others in ways that you yourself would find hurtful.

—Buddhism

Not one of you is a believer until he desires for his brother that which he desires for himself.

—Mohammadism/Islam

This is the sum of duty: Do nothing to others which would cause you pain if done to you.

—Hinduism

From *The Speaker's Sourcebook*, Glenn Van Eheren, Prentice Hall.

THERE WILL BE *Harmony* IN THE HOME.

(Old Chinese poem, owned by Mary Martin, in needlepoint)

If there is *harmony* in the *home*
There will be *order* in the *nation*.
When there is *order* in the *nation*
There will be *peace* in the *world*.

Chapter 1

EFFECTIVE *Introductions* AND *Greetings*

*Good manners is the art of making
people comfortable in our presence.*
—Jonathan Swift

*K*nowing how to introduce people to each other and how to act when you are introduced to someone are important parts of good manners. No one wants to feel self-conscious in a social situation. First impressions are often lasting impressions. Everyone wants to be remembered as friendly, confident, outgoing, kind, and sincere.
A broad smile, eye contact, and a firm handshake are crucial in conveying those attributes.
A smile can be read in any language. It lights up a face and adds warmth to any meeting.

SHAKING hands

Good manners in special circumstances, such as introductions made at a funeral, necessarily dictate a more subdued response. Give the person a sincere, closed-lip smile and then express your condolences to or for the deceased's family, such as, "Mrs. Green, I'm so sorry for your loss. We will all miss Daniel very much," or "Mrs. Green, please accept my condolences. . . . "

- Men shake hands with each other when being introduced.

- Men shake hands with a woman if she extends her hand. (Men, go easy on a woman's hand.)

- Women shake hands with each other if they choose.

- Always use a firm handshake. Not too strong. Not too limp.

HOW TO introduce PEOPLE

MAKING *Introductions*

When meeting new people, always stand up, smile, look the person in the eye, shake hands, and say "How do you do?" using their name ("Sir" or "Ma'am" may be used in place of their name). Don't use their first name without their permission. You may want to save comments like "I am pleased to meet you" or "It was a pleasure meeting you" for later, when you'll be able to say so honestly, but if circumstances seem as if you will not continue in the person's presence, you should express pleasure in meeting him or her immediately after your introduction.

When you are about to be introduced, remove your nonprescription sunglasses (so you can make eye contact), hat (a sign of respect), and gloves (also a sign of respect).

WHEN YOU SHOULDN'T *Shake Hands*

There are times when it is not appropriate or practical for you to shake hands during an introduction. When that is the case, nod your head politely instead.

Some cultures find it rude to make any physical contact *and* eye contact with others. If you expect to meet people from other countries and cultures in your personal or business life, and you probably will someday, take some time to learn about the customs and proper etiquette of other cultures to avoid insulting others inadvertently.

Social *Introductions*

When making social introductions, always introduce a younger person to an older one: "Grandma, this is John Wilson; we're in the same (department/class/club). John, this is my grandmother, Mrs. Jones."

Always introduce a man to a woman. "Susan, this is Mr. David Green, one of my coworkers. David, this is Miss Susan Brown, my good friend." This shows special honor and respect to those of greater age as well as to women and girls.

In a business setting, use courtesy titles consistently. The title "Mr." does not indicate marital status while "Miss" and "Mrs." do. Typically, widows continue to use "Mrs." and divorcées may use "Ms." or "Mrs." Nevertheless, it's wise to know ahead of time which of the single, divorced, widowed, or married women you know prefer the title "Ms." over "Miss" or "Mrs." If you are introduced to a woman and no courtesy title is given, use "Ms." when you address her. In social settings, the use of first and last names is preferred.

Always introduce a boy to a girl. "Sally, this is Joe Gilbert, the captain of our football team. Joe, this is Sally Thomson, my cousin."

If the person you are introducing has a title, be sure to use it as a sign of respect. Whenever possible, add something about the person you are introducing. "Dr. Smith is my dentist." "Neil is my former husband and Tim and Julie's father."

Often introductions take place in large groups amid some confusion, and it can be difficult to remember names. Trying to remember the rules of introductions might add to the confusion. In such circumstances simply concentrate on saying all names loud and clear and take care to pronounce names correctly. That's an important part of any introduction.

If you are not sure how to pronounce a name, simply ask, "I'm sorry, would you repeat your name, please?" Then listen carefully and repeat it.

When you take leave of someone you have just met is the time to say something thoughtful like: "It was a pleasure meeting you" or "It was nice to meet you," using their name.

Introducing YOURSELF

Sometimes there is no one around to introduce you to others. It's perfectly correct to introduce yourself by simply saying, "Hello, I'm Mary Brown."

If the person introducing you seems to suddenly forget your name or how to pronounce it, jump right in and introduce yourself. Don't call attention to their faux pas.

Someday you will meet someone you haven't seen for a long time. Asking "Remember me?" will make you both feel awkward if they don't. Instead, say, "Hello, I'm Jane Brown. It's nice to see you again." If you don't remember their name, say, "I remember speaking with you (say where if you can); I'm sorry, but at the moment I cannot recall your name." Repeat their name and memorize it.

Introducing A GROUP

When a group is small, you can usually introduce each person individually as they arrive, but as the group gets bigger, it gets more difficult. It becomes easier to say, "Friends, I'd like you to meet Peter Green. Peter, this is . . ." (indicate individual people as you mention each name).

Once the group becomes too large for this, or if someone arrives late, simply say, "Friends, this is Peter Green.

Please introduce yourselves to him."

A greeting should be warm and sincere, like: "Betty! It's so good to see you!"

The natural time to start greeting others with enthusiasm is at breakfast with your own family. Greet your family with a hug. Say something to start the day in a positive way, like: "Good morning, (use their name or term of endearment). I hope you're feeling great today," "I hope you had a good night's sleep," "You look nice," or "You look refreshed this morning."

A pleasant smile on your face should be seen as a very natural part of our lifestyle. So be cheerful and act as though it is a pleasure to meet the person.

A *smile* CAN BE READ IN ANY LANGUAGE.

BUSINESS *Introductions*

In business introductions, hierarchy takes precedence over gender and age, and introductions are more formal. In business situations, shaking hands is the only appropriate physical contact between business persons, colleagues, and clients. When spouses, family members, or close friends work together, they should always keep their physical contact and conversations strictly professional in public and in business situations.

Stand up, smile, look the person in the eye, and shake hands. If you're sitting behind a desk, stand up and walk around the desk to greet the visitor.

If your physical ability precludes standing, be sure to welcome the person through your body language as well as by what you say. Put others at ease by making the first gesture if they seem uncertain how to greet you.

Introduce a junior staff member to a superior. "Mr. Samuels, I would like to introduce Ms. Beth Lake from purchasing. Ms. Lake, Mr. Samuels is our senior marketing manager." The trend in business is toward the use of "Ms." unless a woman asks you to address her as Mrs. or Miss.

And always use a married woman's first name in introductions, not her husband's. A married woman who doesn't
use her husband's last name should be called "Ms."

Clients and elected officials outrank even the company
president. "Mr. Collum, I would like to introduce Ms. Day,
our senior accounts executive. Mr. Collum is our client
from XYZ Company in Australia." And, "Governor Knight, I
would like to introduce Ms. Day, our senior accounts
executive."

Know ahead of time if your boss prefers to be
addressed by title and last name in public situations even
if everyone is on a first-name basis at work. If you're not
sure, always use their title and last name to convey the
proper respect.

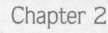

Presenting

YOURSELF

manners matter
manners matter
manners matter
manners matter
manners matter
manners matter
manners matter
manners matter
manners matter

*T*he human body is an absolute miracle. There is no computer equal to the human brain. No camera or lens equal to the human eye. No pump will ever match the human heart. Taking care of your body conveys you're conscientious, responsible, and have good common sense.

healthy LIVING

Eating a balanced diet, exercising to keep fit, and getting enough sleep will help you always be at your best. Healthy food, healthy body—or as the computer people say, "Garbage in, garbage out." People who don't smoke or abuse drugs or alcohol are much healthier than those who do.

People feel and look much healthier when they choose a balanced diet of:

- Fresh fruits and vegetables; low-fat dairy products; whole grains; fish, poultry, and lean meats (for nonvegetarians); plenty of water. . .

- And limit soft drinks, caffeine, sweets, desserts, snack foods, pastries, alcohol, and foods high in cholesterol and fat.

You never get a second chance to make a first impression.

personal HYGIENE

In face-to-face meetings, the first impression that you give is heavily influenced by your personal hygiene. Your charm, wit, intelligence, education, experience, and potential will never be recognized if people you meet cannot look past your bad breath, food lodged between teeth, body odor, pimples, oily or flaky skin and hair, ear wax, smudged eyeglasses, or dirty, tattered clothes. These all put people off—quickly.

four tips to remember:

• Remove your hat whenever you meet someone and when you're indoors—it conveys respect instantly.

• If possible, remove nonprescription sunglasses whenever you meet or greet someone so you can make effective eye contact. (Wearing dark glasses that prevent others from seeing your eyes when indoors will make you look rude, not cool.)

• Being properly groomed conveys a sense of self-respect and that you are worthy of others' respect.

• Practice impeccable personal hygiene to be certain your first impressions will always be your best.

Every day there is a chance you will be making your first impression on someone who may be very important to you someday.

bathing

Shower (or bathe) daily with a good soap, dry off with a clean towel, and always put on clean clothes. A good, ten-minute shower involves shampooing your hair, thoroughly soaping up every part of the body, and rinsing well. Select the type of shampoo and soap  appropriate for your skin type: oily, normal, or dry.

Use a deodorant after you shower. Select one with appropriate strength for your skin type and activity level. Deodorant should never be used as a substitute for bathing or to cover body odor not removed during bathing.

Cologne should add a light scent to a properly cleansed body. Overpowering scents can be nauseating in close quarters and will drive people away. Some people experience allergic reactions to colognes and scents, so go easy.

HAIR care

Groom (clean and condition) your hair at least every other day, daily if your scalp is flaky or oily. When over-the-counter shampoos do not control persistent skin conditions, a physician or dermatologist can suggest more effective treatments.

Have your hair cut or trimmed regularly. A light application of spray, gel, or mousse will keep it tidy. Always touch up your hairstyle, cosmetics, and so on in a rest room, never in public.

shaving

Men and teenage boys should shave and/or groom facial hair daily, generally following bathing. Trim hair that sticks out of your nose or ears.

Women and teenage girls typically shave their legs and underarms while bathing.

tooth AND mouth CARE

Brush your teeth at least twice daily, first thing in the morning and last thing in the evening. If you can do so without gagging yourself, gently brush the upper surface of your tongue to remove residue and bacteria. Carry a travel toothbrush and brush your teeth after meals with plain water if you can't carry a travel size toothpaste with you.

Flossing daily will help keep food particles and bacteria from collecting where toothbrush bristles cannot reach. If you have tightly spaced teeth or wear braces, use floss-threaders or specially designed toothbrushes to cleanse tight spaces.

cosmetics

Women, use scents and makeup sparingly, and only to enhance your features. Avoid leaving lipstick smudges on napkins or cups by blotting after application; generally, apply all cosmetics in the rest room, rather than in public. Lipsticks may be applied in public, if handled discreetly.

skin AND nail CARE

Use moisturizers to soften rough or dry skin. Use sunscreen with an SPF rating of at least 15 to prevent skin damage that leads to premature aging and skin cancer.

Keep your fingernails and toenails impeccably clean. Trim toenails weekly. File down sharp nail edges, cuticles, and calluses on hands and feet.

Men and boys, keep your fingernails short. Clean under your nails after working outdoors and doing household projects.

Women and girls, keep your fingernails short enough that nails don't interfere with efficiency in performing tasks. If you wear nail polish, choose a color suitable for your daily environment and remove chipped nail polish promptly.

PIERCED skin AND jewelry

Thoroughly disinfect and sterilize pierced earlobes (or

any pierced site) and the jewelry you wear in them every day. Even if you leave your jewelry in place all the time, it's wise to disinfect the skin and jewelry after bathing.

clothes

Wear clean clothes that are in good condition, and keep your shoes and accessories like belts, handbags, briefcases, and so on, clean and in good condition.

What you wear speaks volumes about you. Dressing appropriately merely means choosing attire that is suitable for the situation *and* for you, fits properly, is of reasonably good quality (making it last longer), and shows good taste.

Good manners display modesty, as well, so choose clothes that fit well enough that they do not reveal your undergarments or too much skin, are not skintight, or appear loose enough to fall off. Choose wisely what your attire "says" about your manners.

Old, comfortable shoes are fine as long as they don't *look* old. Replace items that are frayed, badly worn or scuffed, smell bad, or are visibly damaged beyond repair. Dedicate your comfortable, tattered clothes and shoes for use when painting the house, gardening, or working on the car. (Tip: If you go after more supplies in midproject, wash up and change your clothes to avoid getting paint, dirt, or grease inside your vehicle or elsewhere.)

glasses AND hats

Eyeglasses, sunglasses, hats, and gloves should also be kept clean and in good condition.

fashion TRENDS

While it's true that "you can't judge a book by its cover," most people equate style extremes with rebellion and a disrespect for others and for oneself. Justified or not, body piercing, tattoos, neon hair colors, wild hairstyles and cosmetics, heavy chains, gaudy jewelry, audacious or immodest clothing, or a wardrobe that consists of black leather and rivets will usually undermine the wearer's credibility.

On the other hand, don't be too hasty to judge others who express themselves through unusual styles. Plenty of decent, mannerly individuals wear bold styles in order to be seen as unique. And impeccably groomed individuals could be the worst kind of villains in disguise.

Whatever you do, consider the consequences carefully. Tattoos and body piercing leave permanent marks and scars you may someday regret. Going to a job interview sporting a tattoo, nose ring, or pierced eyebrow may disqualify you before the interview begins.

Fashion is a personal choice. Using good "fashion" manners will help open the door to important opportunities.

posture

Did you ever notice that you sit and stand taller when you feel good than when you feel bad? There's more zip in your movements when you feel good; your attitude is better, and there's more confidence in your voice.

Weak posture suggests weakness, fosters disrespect, impairs speaking ability, and turns people off. It decreases stature, weakens self-esteem, and invites failure.

Strong posture requires discipline but suggests you

have it all together, displays strength, and influences a better mental outlook. It also increases your stature, enhances your personal appeal, and helps your clothes fit better.

PERSONAL values

As important as it is to be presentable on the outside, it's more important to have "presentable" values. Everything a person says and does literally presents their internal value system to others.

Morally or spiritually impure habits and activities can scar or destroy an individual's value system and life—just like pollutants in the environment destroy wildlife and habitats.

Avoiding these dangers is seldom easy. People are bombarded with sounds and images that make harmful things seem exciting. Choose to listen to your built-in alarm system—your conscience. Remember that no one ever became very wicked all at once.

danger SIGNS

Entertainment that promotes violence, intolerance, or promiscuity

X-rated movies and pornographic magazines

Drugs, including alcohol, nicotine, and mind-altering substances

Dirty jokes and demeaning or offensive language

Harmful habits and negative attitudes

WHEN IN doubt

golden RULE

FOLLOW THE GOLDEN RULE: "DO TO OTHERS AS YOU WOULD HAVE THEM DO TO YOU."

ESTABLISH HIGH STANDARDS FOR YOURSELF.

ASK, "WOULD I WANT MY FAMILY OR SOME-ONE I RESPECT TO SEE ME DOING THIS?"

Respect

BE WILLING TO SAY "NO," EVEN IF EVERYONE ELSE IS DOING IT.

No

DISCUSS THINGS YOU FIND QUESTIONABLE WITH PEOPLE WHOSE VALUES YOU RESPECT.

TELL THE TRUTH.

values

Truth

CHOOSING THE right FRIENDS

True friends will have the same values as you and do things that you, your family, or others you respect would approve of. End friendships that are unhealthy.

YOUR home

Your home environment tells more about you than a mirror. Are you neat or raunchy? Do you care what kind of impression you make? Is your life in order? Or in disorder?

Guests should be able to see furniture surfaces, walk without tripping, sit without moving discarded articles, and relax in a clean, inviting, pleasant-smelling environment.

Most teenagers' rooms have stereos that are often more important than the beds. It's a nice display of manners to make the volume level as comfortable

as the bed. Someone in the next room may be trying to read. In extreme cases, someone on the next block may be trying to concentrate.

Parents, how clean and tidy you keep your home may seem to have no influence on your children now. Setting a good example will make a difference—someday.

Chapter 3

TABLE *Manners* AND DINNER *Parties*

*D*id you ever stop to think about how much of our social interaction revolves around food? It only makes sense to be sure of "the rules" as they apply to such occasions—from the time an invitation arrives to the moment dessert is over.

DINNER party INVITATIONS

Whether a dinner invitation arrives by mail or telephone, a prompt reply is always considerate.

Formal written invitations may say "RSVP," an abbreviation for the French words *répondez s'il vous plaît* meaning "Reply If You Please." Reply to these invitations whether you are able to attend or not.

If the invitation says, "Regrets only," it means just that.

If you accept an invitation and later discover you cannot attend, notify the host and hostess as soon as possible.

If you have a severe, life-threatening allergy to some particular food, especially if it is likely to be the main course (entrée), it is best to tell the hostess when you call to accept the invitation. If it is a side dish, you can merely abstain from taking some. Let your hostess know if you're a vegetarian or have special dietary needs so she can adapt the menu if necessary.

Be prompt but do not arrive more than five or ten minutes early. If you find that you will be more than fifteen minutes late, call and notify your hostess with a sincere apology.

PRE-DINNER social TIME

hints:

- Don't set your glass down on a table without using a coaster.

- Any pits, stems, or other disposables should be put into a napkin unless another way of disposing of them is provided.

- With dips, only dip once per chip.

- Never place your glasses, keys, and such on the side tables or dinner table.

Often before dinner the hostess will serve beverages and hors d'oeuvres (appetizers). This gives guests time to gather and introduce themselves to one another.

You can be sure the hostess has spent a lot of time and effort on the meal. By practicing good table manners at home, you will know what is expected and feel comfortable in more formal circumstances.

Food is served several different ways at dinner parties:

family STYLE:

After everyone is seated, the food is passed around the table in serving dishes. Sometimes the host or hostess will serve the meat dish.

buffet STYLE:

The food is placed on a serving table. If it is a large party, guests help themselves and occasionally eat off their laps or small tables.

formal STYLE:

A waiter or waitress brings the serving dishes to each person at the table, or the food is placed on the plates elsewhere and brought to you at the table.

table SETTINGS

formal dinner SETTING

goblet

appetizer or soup

butter plate

dessert fork

salad plate

cup and saucer

fish – salad – dinner fork

dinner plate

knife

dinner teaspoon

soup spoon

The way forks, knives, spoons, glasses, and cups are placed on the table is a "table setting."

The one shown here is a *formal* place setting for a full course dinner. Most people don't use all of this each day at home. However, it shows where each piece is placed, whether there are eight pieces of silver or three.

Use the silver from the *outside in*. For example, the soup spoon on the right would be used before the tea-spoon, because soup is served first.

Use the glass to the right of your plate. Large stemmed glasses are called *goblets*. Hold by the bowl, not the stem, to avoid spills. Hold a glass without a stem in the middle, not at the rim.

If you need to pass a glass or cup to someone, don't touch its rim with your fingers.

Although table settings will vary, depending on where you are eating, use good table manners at all times.

At a buffet, plates are usually stacked at the beginning of the serving table. Sometimes the silverware is wrapped in napkins on the serving table; other times, it will be at your table.

A spoon or fork placed above the dinner plate is used for dessert.

If the setting is confusing, just watch the hostess and use what she uses. If you begin to use the wrong utensil, don't worry about it—just continue to use it for that course.

Your bread-and-butter plate is located on your left, slightly above your plate. Use this plate for rolls, butter, olive pits, and so forth. Your butter knife will be on this plate and should be left there after you use it.

Your salad plate is also to the left of your dinner plate, slightly below the bread-and-butter plate. Generally salad is eaten first so the salad fork is to the left of the dinner fork.

informal dinner
SETTING

When you sit at the table, place your napkin on your lap immediately.

- A large dinner napkin is opened in half with the fold on top. The open bottom half may be used to blot your mouth.

- Open the napkin as you place it on your lap, don't flap it like a flag.

- A small luncheon napkin may be opened all the way.

- Remember, a napkin isn't meant to be a bib, towel, or handkerchief. Never blow your nose in a napkin. Use napkins to blot or wipe your mouth.

- Sit up straight with your hands on your lap, not on the table.

- Don't rock or tip your chair.

- Keep your feet to yourself, flat on the floor under your chair or cross them at the ankles. No kicking or sprawling.

The napkin is either folded or slipped through a napkin ring and placed to the left of the plate or in the center of the plate. On occasion the napkin will be folded decoratively and placed in your glass or coffee cup, which is to the right of your plate.

Chargers have become popular today in many more formal homes or restaurants. A charger is always left on the table and is made of a different materials than china and more decorative. Your service plates and others go on top of the charger.

When you are called to the table, the hostess will indicate where you should sit, unless there are formal place cards by each plate.

Stand behind your chair at the table until the hostess is seated or asks you to sit.

Men should assist the woman next to them to be seated by pulling out her chair and easing it back toward the table.

WHEN YOU SIT AT THE *table*, PLACE YOUR *napkin* ON YOUR LAP IMMEDIATELY.

ENJOYING THE meal

Many people precede their meals with a prayer of thanks. It may be referred to as "grace," "the blessing," or "returning thanks." The food will be present but not served until the hostess is seated and she or the host says the prayer.

Remember to wait for your hostess to lift her fork before you begin to eat—or until she tells you to begin.

At a large dinner party of more than eight to twelve, you may begin to eat after four or five people have been served.

Forks and spoons are held more like a pencil than a shovel, and it's not polite to wipe silverware clean with your napkin (if it really needs it, wipe it discreetly, under the table).

Talk to the person seated next to you at the table as you eat—but not when your mouth is full. Dinner-table conversation should be light and pleasant. Don't get into arguments or describe your knee surgery in gory detail.

bread-AND-butter PLATE

- Rolls, bread, butter, or jelly are all placed on the bread-and-butter plate.

- Break off a small piece of bread or roll and butter it. Never slice it.

  - As you eat, take butter from only one end of the stick and place a small amount on your bread-and-butter plate.

  - Take the roll closest to you when they are passed. Don't thumb through them.

soup

- Spoon soup away from you. When it's near the bottom of the bowl, tilt the bowl away from you to spoon up the rest.

  - If soup is too hot, skim from the top or side of the bowl. Never blow on your soup and never slurp.

- Sip from the side of the spoon, not the point. Don't put the spoon in your mouth.

- Leave the spoon in the bowl when resting. When you're finished, put the spoon on the plate underneath.

  - If soup is served in a cup, spoon the first few tastes, then if you wish, you may drink the rest and place the spoon on the plate below.

  - Never drink from a mug or cup with your spoon still in it.

passing FOOD

- Unless the hostess indicates otherwise, pass food counterclockwise (to your right).

- Never touch the rim of a cup or glass when passing it.

  - As serving dishes are passed, use the serving utensil provided. Return the utensil to the serving dish before passing it on. Never use your own fork or spoon to help yourself.

- Take moderate portions that leave plenty for other guests. Only take as much as you intend to eat.

- You should take a little of everything whether you like it or not (unless you have a severe food allergy). Never ask, "What's this?" You can leave something on your plate, but be polite about it.

- If you would like seconds after everyone has been served, either ask politely and pass your plate (leaving your fork and knife pointing into the center of the plate so they don't fall off) or ask to have the food passed to you.

- Pass items to someone who has asked for them, but don't help yourself first. Ask them to pass the dish back if you want some.

- Pace yourself so you finish about the same time as everyone else.

- Hold your fork in your left hand, tines down, and cut with the knife in your right hand, bearing down as you cut. And cut only one or two pieces at a time as you eat.

• If food is tough, use a short, sawing motion and cut into very small pieces.

• Don't make wings of your elbows as you cut.

• Salad greens may be cut if they seem too large.

• Fried chicken is finger food on a picnic but is cut with a knife and fork in a dining room unless the hostess gives permission otherwise.

GENERAL table MANNERS

• Sit up straight and bring your food to your mouth, not your mouth to your food.

• Remove the empty fork or spoon from your mouth, leaving the entire bite in your mouth.

• Feed yourself with one hand and leave the other on your lap.

• Take small bites and drink slowly.

• Gravy may be enjoyed by using a small piece of bread or roll to sop it up with.

- Slice a baked potato down the middle with your knife. Pinch the potato with both hands to open it, then season to taste.

- Use the tip of your knife or a small piece of bread to push small bits of food onto your fork.

- Silverware or flatware should never touch the table once you've picked them up; keep them on your plate.

- Rest one hand in your lap and the other wrist at the table edge when not eating; don't put your elbows on or lean on the table at any time.

- No matter how they beg, don't feed pets at the table.

- When you are finished, place your knife and fork together in the center of your plate, tips pointing down. This tells the waiter that you are finished and keeps the utensils from falling on the floor when the plate is picked up.

awkwardness

- Keep your tongue inside your mouth when you take a bite.

- Never chew with your mouth open. Chew quietly. Please, don't chew ice.

- Never talk with food in your mouth.

- If something is too hot, never spit it out. The best remedy is a quick sip of cold water.

- Never gesture with food in your hands or on your utensils.

- If something is stuck in a tooth, it's best ignored until after the meal, or ask to be excused and remove it elsewhere. Toothpicks are acceptable at home, but not in public. Fingers are never acceptable toothpicks.

- If you need to attend to something personal, ask to be excused without any announcements. "May I be excused for a moment, please?" will do. Place your napkin on your chair, not on the table.

• If you forgot to remove an orthodontic appliance, excuse yourself to do so. Remove and replace it in the rest room, never in public. Wash your hands before returning.

• If blowing your nose is necessary, generally excuse yourself from the table; in a spontaneous necessity, take care of the matter discreetly.

• If a belch, cough, or sneeze is imminent, shield your mouth and nose with your napkin if you have no tissue or handkerchief, keep your mouth closed if you can, and turn your head toward your shoulder. Quietly say "Excuse me" and go on. Don't call attention to gastrointestinal surprises.

• Hiccups unfortunately demand attention. Keep your mouth closed when you hiccup. Taking several consecutive swallows of water may help.

• If you spill something on the table, apologize and offer to help clean it up, but don't die of embarrassment.

• If you spill something on a person, apologize and offer to pay their cleaning bill, but don't touch the person or their clothes! Don't prolong your mutual embarrassment.

• Before squeezing any food that might squirt, cup one hand around it, just in case.

• A pit, bone, or a piece of gristle may be removed with fingertips or the tip of your fork and placed on the side of the dinner or bread and butter plate. Never spit anything out.

• If you need to remove something from your mouth, remember: If it went in by hand. . .take it out by hand. If it went in by fork. . .take it out by fork.

dessert

- Ice cream or other soft desserts are eaten with spoons. When you are done, leave the spoon on the plate under the ice cream dish.

- Ice cream served with cake or pie may be eaten with a fork.

- If nuts or after-dinner mints are passed, take a few and put them on your plate. Don't eat out of the serving bowl!

- Fruit centerpieces are not meant to be eaten unless offered by the hostess.

AFTER THE meal

- Thank the hostess (or host) and compliment them on the meal.

- Offer to help clean up.

- When you leave the table, place your napkin at the side of your plate (don't refold it) and push your chair back under the table.

Chapter 4

Restaurant
MANNERS

manners matter manners matter manners matter manners matter

*E*veryone enjoys going out to eat. You can assume that everyone else in the restaurant is there for a pleasant experience, too. Be considerate of those around you and those who serve you.

The table manners discussed in the preceding chapter all apply to restaurant dining, too.

- Never place cell phones, keys, glasses, or any other personal items on the table. The only things that belong on the table are those provided for serving and eating the meal.

  - Put a handbag behind you on your chair (but not hanging from the chair back) or put it slightly under the chair where no one will trip over it.

    - When you order, be courteous.

    - When you're served, say, "thank you" to the waiter or server.

  - Always control the level of your voice.

There are basically four types of *restaurants*.

FAST *food*   *cafeteria*

family RESTAURANT   *gourmet* RESTAURANT

fast-food RESTAURANTS

- Know exactly what you want to order before reaching the head of the line, especially if there are a lot of people waiting behind you.

- Take only the amount of napkins, straws, and condiments that you'll need.

- If there is no place mat at your table, open a napkin and place your food on it for sanitary reasons.

- Sometimes a place mat is placed on a food tray for that purpose.

- Collect your trash and dispose of it in the bin provided as you leave.

~~~

cafeteria

- In a cafeteria it's helpful to know what is available and make your decisions before reaching the serving line. This keeps things moving, especially when there are others behind you.

• When you reach your table with your food and silverware, "set your place" as you would at home.

• Keep your tray to bus your table if the cafeteria has no one assigned to do this. Otherwise take your tray to a nearby tray stand.

family RESTAURANTS

• Family restaurants offer sit-down dinners. You are shown to a table and given a menu. A waiter takes your order and brings the food to you. Family restaurants have a larger selection than fast-food restaurants and are more affordable than gourmet restaurants.

•Silverware will be at the table wrapped in a napkin or placed on an open napkin or will be brought to the table once you are seated. Set the silverware out as you would when eating at home.

• If a bread-and-butter plate is not provided, place them on your dinner plate, never on the bare table.

• Place empty cracker wrappers or butter papers under your plate.

• When you need to get your server's attention, call them "Waiter" or "Waitress" not "Mister," "Sir," "Miss," or "Ma'am." Never tap your glass, snap your fingers, wave or clap your hands, or above all, whistle to get their attention.

salad BARS

• Never use your fingers to take anything from a salad bar.

• Be as careful as possible to avoid spilling the salad selections you choose.

• If one food accidentally falls into another, carefully replace it with the tongs.

- Don't take more than you can eat or pile your plate too full.

- Select the bread or roll you want without handling the others.

gourmet RESTAURANTS

Gourmet restaurants deserve the "fine dining" description. The food, décor, atmosphere, and service are all finer than in other restaurants. The prices are also higher.

None of these qualities necessarily make gourmet restaurants "better," they simply offer a different dining experience. In a fine restaurant, a maître d' will show you to your table, a busboy will fill your water glass and serve rolls, and a waiter or waitress will take your order and serve you. In upscale restaurants, your waiter will place your napkin in your lap.

Making reservations is a good idea. If you cannot keep a reservation, call to cancel. If you decide to add more to your party, inform the restaurant before arriving.

Wear "dressier" clothes in gourmet restaurants. You'll definitely feel more comfortable and enjoy your visit more.

If you are invited as a guest, be considerate. Don't order the most expensive item on the menu. Wait to see, for example, if your host orders an appetizer, soup, salad, or dessert. All of these items increase the total bill significantly. If your host does not order extra items, be considerate and don't order them, either.

The service staff will be happy to explain menu items you don't understand. If you drop your silverware, leave it on the floor and ask for a replacement. It's not necessary or sanitary to pick up dropped utensils.

WHEN YOU'RE SERVED, SAY *thank you* TO THE WAITER OR SERVER.

THE menu

There are two basic types of food service in a restaurant:

- *Table d'hôte:* one price for a complete meal

- *À la carte:* each course is priced separately

Read your menu carefully or inquire before ordering, if you're in doubt. A full meal includes an appetizer, soup, salad, main course (entrée), dessert, and beverage. If you know you can't eat that much, ask to skip one or two courses, or order à la carte. Many restaurants include a salad and a vegetable with the entrée. Feel free to inquire.

Many finer restaurants offer a small sorbet (sherbet) after the salad course. This chills the taste buds and clears the salad flavor for the main course, but it usually comes as a surprise to most diners.

If crackers are served with the soup course, no matter what you do at home, this is not the time to crumble up the crackers and drown them in your soup.

If your fingers become sticky, wet the corner of your napkin in your water glass and use it to clean your fingers.

don't

- Use straws or sweetener packages for creative activities.

- Dangle spoons from your nose, play music with glasses, or crunch ice.

- Pile dishes or assist in cleaning the table.

- Write on tablecloths or write anything in a rest room.

- Cut bread with small bread-and-butter knife.

- Get carried away with the ketchup bottle or use your knife to get it started.

rest ROOMS

- The fewer items you touch in a rest room, the better.

- Always flush, wash your hands, and place towels in receptacles.

- Leave the rest room neat.

THE check AND tipping

Review the check carefully for accuracy. Some restaurants automatically include the gratuity, or tip (also known as surcharge). You wouldn't want to overlook this detail and tip twice, regardless of how good the service may have been.

The standard tip is 15 percent. Some people tip 18 percent or 20 percent if they feel the service has been very special. If your waiter has given extremely poor service, you may want to adjust the quantity of your tip accordingly or mention it to the management. Very bad service typically results in a 10 percent tip. Blatantly rude service deserves none.

If you are served a meal that is clearly unacceptable, good manners do not require you to eat it. You could do yourself and the management a favor by calling it to their attention. All well-operated restaurants will gladly replace the unsatisfactory food or make a suitable adjustment.

THE STANDARD *Tip* IS 15 PERCENT.

miscellaneous

Formal restaurants have a plate at each place or will put one there after guests are seated. This is the "service plate." Appetizer, salad, or soup plates are placed on this service plate. The service plate is removed when the entrée is served.

Folks who are diet conscious may choose to share a dessert. Your waiter will be happy to bring one dessert and two plates. This way you can have your cake and eat it, too.

Tea is usually served in the form of a tea bag with a pot of hot water. Place the tea bag in the teapot (not your cup) allow it to brew to the strength you want. Leave the tag on the outside of the teapot.

Remove the tea bag with your spoon, wrapping the string around it, draining water into the pot. Place the tea bag on your saucer or service plate. When the tea bag is served by the side of your cup, handle it the same way when it is removed.

finger BOWL

A fine restaurant will serve a finger bowl after dinner. Dip your fingers, one hand at a time, into the bowl and dry them on your napkin.

If a piece of lemon is in the water, rub your fingers with it to remove any lingering food odors. You may touch your fingers to your lips if necessary and dry them with your napkin.

DO I EAT IT WITH A
Fork, Spoon, OR *Fingers?*

Fresh grapes, plums, cherries,
celery, carrot sticks . . . . Fingers

Pickles, olives, radishes . . . . Fingers

Corn on the cob . . . . Fingers

French fries (fast-food, picnic) . . . . Fingers

French fries (dining room) . . . . Fork

Fried chicken (picnic) . . . . Fingers

Fried chicken (dining room) . . . . Fork

Watermelon. . . . . Fork

Strawberries or dessert. . . . . Fork

Cut fruit on dinner plate . . . . Fork

Dry, crisp bacon . . . . May be eaten with fingers

Artichoke . . . . Pull each leaf
with fingers to dip in butter

Lobster in shell . . . . Parts can only be eaten
with fingers

Foreign WORDS ON MENU

à la. . . . . in the style of

à la au glaise . . . . cooked in liquid

à la carte . . . . menu whereby each course is priced separately

à la king . . . . in cream sauce

almandine. . . . . with almonds

asperges. . . . . asparagus

au jus . . . . in its own juice

au lait . . . . with milk

béchamel . . . . white sauce

beurre d'ail. . . . . garlic butter

béarnaise sauce. . . . . sauce with tarragon

bisque . . . . . . a type of soup, usually seafood

boeuf . . . . beef

boeuf bourguignon . . . . beef cooked with
burgundy wine (type of stew)

bonbon . . . . candy

bordelaise. a brown sauce

bouillabaisse. . . . . fish chowder

braisé . . . . braised

brioche. . . . . a French yeast roll

cafe glacé . . . . coffee ice cream

calamari. . . . . squid

calmar. . . . . squid

canapé . . . . small open-faced sandwich

canard. . . . . duck

cassaulet. . . . . type of stew

champignons . . . . mushroom

citron. . . . . lemon

compote de fruits . . . . stewed fruit
(served hot or cold)

consommé. . . . . clear soup (broth)
made from well-seasoned meat or chicken

If you must answer a call, be courteous to your first caller by saying something like, "I'm sorry, Kelly, that's the repair shop calling. I should take that call. Would you like me to call you back?" If Kelly says she'll wait, deal with the other call quickly. If it's an important call that can't wait and may take longer than thirty seconds, ask the second caller, "Would you excuse me briefly while I end my other call? Thank you." Then switch back to "Kelly" and end the call politely. When you return to either caller, thank them for waiting.

wireless COMMUNICATIONS

Technology is intended to make our lives better. Don't abuse your relationships by misusing devices and services designed for convenience.

There's nothing unmannerly about wireless communication devices; however, the buzz in many public places is righteous indignation over how they are used.

The ringing or chirping of phones, pagers, watches, and other devices is unwelcome in churches, theaters, restaurants, meetings, and in audiences of any kind including school concerts, classes, parties, and ceremonies (especially weddings and funerals).

audiences

If you expect an urgent call while you're in an audience, sit in the back with your phone set for a silent mode so you can leave without disturbing others. If you have an assigned seat, let your voice mail take a message and return the call when you reach the lobby. If you forget to silence your phone and it rings while you're in an audience, silence it quickly, even if you have to shut it off. Dim bright display screens in dark places.

courtesy FOR COMPANIONS

Wireless phone services that offer incoming calls free are doing a disservice to people in face-to-face settings. It may be great for customers to know you will always answer their call, as well as for your budget. But it is rude to everyone else including the customer you place on hold to answer the next free incoming call.

Don't put your wireless phone or other electronic devices on the table during a meeting—whether it's casual or formal, personal or business. Putting your wireless phone on display suggests an air of self-importance and tells the people you're with they aren't worth your full attention.

The interruption of a phone call or pager can seem downright rude to your companions. If you expect an important call, let them know in advance. Excuse yourself before taking a call and explain why it was urgent (to the extent appropriate, but spare the details). Caller ID and text messaging may minimize interruptions, *unless* you're constantly looking at your phone instead of your companions.

Keep your private phone conversations private and do not subject the people around you to the details of your personal life. Don't scold someone over the phone, whether it's your child or someone who works for you, and keep conversations that others will overhear quiet and polite.

Restaurants, even fast-food restaurants, are not telephone booths. Many phone booths are still fairly soundproof for good reason. The enclosure keeps the conversation private and the ambient noise from overwhelming your call.

When waiting in line to be served, end calls before it's your turn so you won't delay the server or people behind you. Don't answer your phone while someone is serving you.

Two-way radios are still commonly used. Unless you are a law enforcement officer or other emergency personnel, don't broadcast in public places.

Never ask to borrow a wireless phone unless it's urgent or an emergency. Then keep it brief. Air-time and "free" minutes get used up quickly, and you put the phone's owner "on the sidelines" while you're on their phone.

Caution: Radio frequency scanners can monitor conversations on wireless phones or cordless phones within certain frequency ranges. And wireless Internet access is not yet secure. Consider using a corded, landline phone when giving someone your credit card number or other identifying information.

COMMUTING WITH
courtesy

When you're driving, let your voice mail take a message or pull over and stop before you answer. Then stay put until you're finished with your call. If it isn't safe to stop, resist the temptation to talk on the phone while you drive.

Keep your voice low so you don't interfere with announcements in airports, train stations, bus depots, or on public transportation. You might miss the announcement, but others shouldn't have to. (If you're polite, they might tell you what you missed.)

Some commuters like the quiet time to read and relax. If you must call someone while riding public transportation, keep it brief and quiet.

Keep your voice low for the person you are speaking to on the phone, as well. The microphones in today's wireless phones are extremely sensitive. Shouting into the phone will not improve its reception.

RESIST THE *temptation* TO TALK ON THE PHONE WHILE YOU *drive.*

electronic TOOLS AND entertainment

The high-tech market offers a rapidly expanding, vast array of electronic devices beyond two-way radios, wireless phones, and pagers. Media players, pocket-sized electronic games, watches with stock quotes, electronic day planners, and notebook PCs that connect to the Internet via wireless connections are becoming more and more prevalent.

Many of these devices come with sound effects that you may find charming and entertaining, but they are often annoying to others. Whether these gadgets are exciting entertainment or practical, indispensable tools, manners matter when using them.

With all electronic games and media players, keep the volume low so you don't disturb neighbors or fellow commuters, and be polite about the media content you choose. Others should not be able to hear your earphones, and please don't wriggle or make distracting sounds.

Shut devices off and remove earphones when you are in an audience, class, or talking with someone. When you're wearing earphones, the volume of *your* voice will increase dramatically. (And if you sing, you might be off-key!)

Chapter 8

Family MANNERS
FOR *Kids* OF ALL AGES

The best time to tackle a minor problem is before it grows up.

Where there is life, there should be love. Especially family love. Love makes a house a home. Size, color, and location have nothing to do with the spirit that dwells inside.

A family and its manners are shaped by the quality of the spirit they share. A spirit based on love makes a happy home and always produces good manners.

When a child feels love, understanding, and genuine recognition, many of the problems of delinquency are avoided.

Manners aren't taught in school. Children learn manners at home. They study their parents. The learning process begins in the cradle. It's quickly evident that a child doesn't have to be *taught* to be bad. They have to be taught to be *good*. If a parent doesn't teach, a child will tend to go as far as he can. . .in the wrong direction.

Children learn best by example. They mimic what they see. The parent who loves always teaches and trains. A lack of discipline signifies a lack of love.

CHILDREN LEARN BEST BY *example.*

MANY LESSONS IN life ARE
caughtNOTtaught

If a child lives with criticism,

He learns to condemn.

If a child lives with hostility,

He learns to fight.

If a child lives with ridicule,

He learns to be shy.

If a child lives with shame,

He learns to feel guilty.

If a child lives with tolerance,

He learns to be patient.

If a child lives with encouragement,

He learns confidence.

If a child lives with praise,

He learns to appreciate.

If a child lives with fairness,

He learns justice.

If a child lives with security,

He learns to have faith.

If a child lives with approval,
He learns to like himself.
If a child lives with acceptance
and friendship, he learns to
find love in the world.

Second in importance to love in a family is communication. Families need to talk to each other, and they need
to talk honestly.

It's not always easy to be completely honest. Some
subjects are embarrassing to discuss. It might seem easier, at times, to tell a "white lie" and avoid the truth.
Honesty is always the best policy and the best manners,
especially at home.

Good manners are healthy and make us good listeners.
A family can't enjoy communication if no one is listening. It
may seem easier to "speak up" than to *listen*. Manners can
become sloppy. We relax a bit too much. People living in
close quarters can sometimes rub each other the wrong
way. We're all vulnerable to hurt and upset.

Don't forget that love is a very unselfish quality of life.
Don't forget all about good manners or think selfishly.

Look for balm rather than blame. The closeness that causes friction in a home shouldn't overshadow the closeness that makes a family. Family love, support, and forgiveness are far greater than any hurts.

No one *knows* you like a *brother,*
No one *loves* you like a *mother,*
No one *trusts* you like a *sister,*
No one *cares* for you like a *father.*

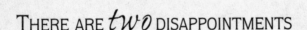

There are *two* disappointments in *life:*
1. Not getting *everything* we want.
2. Getting *everything* we want.
—Mark Twain

It naturally hurts to be corrected or denied something we want very badly, but the biggest handicap parents can impose on a child is to make life too easy.

A parent may need to withhold many things, but never love. A child may need to accept limits on his desires, but always in love.

DON'T BE *discouraged* IF YOUR CHILDREN *reject* YOUR ADVICE. YEARS LATER THEY WILL OFFER IT TO THEIR OWN *offspring*.

- Have a positive attitude. Be cheerful, honest, and try to get along.

- Don't try to manipulate or "guilt" others into doing something.

- Be direct and polite when you need to discuss a conflict, whether between parent and child or between other family members. It's good training for solving conflicts encountered outside the family.

- Pitch in with chores and tasks; keep bathrooms and common rooms clean when you leave the room; help a little extra when someone is sick or injured.

• Ask permission before borrowing things, promptly return them to where you found them, and return them in the same or better condition than when you borrowed them; immediately make amends if you lose or damage something you borrowed.

• Don't insist others borrow something of yours and then resent it when they don't return the item promptly.

• Avoid disgusting habits like:

♦ picking at your face, nose, teeth, hair, beard, mustache, ears or earrings, scalp, acne, scabs, or any other body part—especially around food and drinks

♦ snorting, spitting, cracking knuckles, passing gas

♦ belching, sneezing, or coughing without covering your mouth and nose

♦ clearing your throat noisily, sniffling, or blowing your nose at the table (preferably done in private in bathroom)

- chewing gum with your mouth open

- smoking

- bouncing your leg up and down or vibrating your foot nervously

  - scratching yourself or brushing off dust or dandruff anywhere near where people prepare or eat food or drinks

  - brushing or combing your hair or applying makeup or lipstick in public

  - resting an uncovered or bandaged wound on a counter, table, or other surface

baby-sitting

Children are like mosquitoes — the
minute they stop making noises you
know they're getting into something.

As baby-sitters, you're in charge of much more than diapers, bottles and toys. . .you're in charge of life.

Baby-sitting is one of the most
important jobs in the world.
When you're asked to baby-sit,
you're being paid far more than a
fee! You're being paid a tremendous
compliment. Parents are trusting you
with their most valuable possessions. . .
their children and their home.

Whether parents say it or not, they're actually telling
every baby-sitter they believe you're honest, trustworthy,
capable, responsible, intelligent, loving, qualified, and
compassionate.

It gives you a lot to think about, doesn't it? Don't fall
short.

Before the parents leave you need to know what
exactly you are expected to do.

In an *emergency,* you should *know:*

- Where the parents can be reached.

- A neighbor's phone number.

- The street address in case 911 is called.

- The phone numbers for fire and police if there's
no 911 service.

- The family doctor's phone number.

- Where to find the child's medication for asthma, diabetes, or severe allergies.

OLDER *children:*

- Are the children permitted to play outside? Have company?

- Are they allowed to go swimming? Should they bathe before bedtime?

- Are they to be fed? Can they watch TV? Play video games? For how long?

- Program restrictions? Is there homework? Can they have snacks?

Babies:

- Does the baby need a bottle? Should bottle be warmed? How?

- Does the baby need more than a bottle? What? When? How much?

- Where are the diapers? What is the baby's bedtime routine?

house CARE

Your first responsibility is to the children, but you're also responsible for the house. You're expected to care for both.

Clean up after the children, keep toys picked up, leave the kitchen neat, and clean any dishes you use. Leave the house looking as good or better than when you arrived.

Don't use the phone, have friends in, leave the house, help yourself to food and drinks, or use any media or electronic equipment without the parents' prior permission.

If someone calls for the parents, take a message. Say they cannot come to the phone, but don't reveal that you're the baby-sitter and the parents are not home. Write down who called, their number, when they called, and any message. Give the message to the parents when they return.

MANNERS FOR
YOUNGER *Kids*

birthday PARTIES

Birthday parties are fun! They mean presents, cards, games, friends, cake and ice cream, and all sorts of neat decorations. They also mean you're a year older and at a perfect time to display your manners.

WHEN *you* ARE THE *host*

Spend as much time as possible with each guest at your party. Don't show any favoritism when you're the host. Greet each person and be sure to introduce them to anyone they don't know.

- Thank each one with lots of enthusiasm for their gift.

  - If you don't like a gift you receive, don't reveal it.

- If you already have the very same thing, don't reveal that, either.

  - It's nice go to the door with each guest as they leave. Thank them again for the gift. (Try to name the gift.)

WHEN *you* ARE A *guest*

  - If the birthday child [person] answers the door, always wish them a "happy birthday" and be sure to add their name as you present your birthday gift.

  - If you're met at the door by someone you haven't met, introduce yourself.

    - Participate in all the games and enjoy them.

    - Use all your good manners at the table and during the party.

    - When you leave the party, thank your friend and his or her parents [if appropriate] for a special time.

    - Leave them one of your best smiles.

Always BE ON *time!*

Birthday parties are very special events. Arriving on time is polite and important. Your friend who is celebrating can't wait for the fun to begin. The parents have been filling balloons, decorating, baking a cake, and putting plenty of love and effort into all the preparations. All you have to do is to be on time and let the fun begin!

HONOR YOUR parents AND grandparents

Parents deserve your respect. They don't need to *qualify* for it—they earned it when they gave you life. Honor your parents by asking for their advice, looking at things from their perspective, trying to please them, having a good attitude, and showing respect. Thank your parents, compliment them, and obey them.

Parents need your honor. They want to know they have your support, just as you want to know you have theirs.

Take out the garbage, do the dishes, volunteer to do

chores. Better yet, do chores without complaining! Have a grateful attitude, a cheerful, cooperative spirit—this will help parents the most.

Respect your grandparents; write to them. Always remember to thank them, and tell them you love them.

sisters AND brothers

We often spend more time with our sisters and brothers than we do with anyone else. We also may have more problems with them than we have with others!

Manners show in the way you speak to those you love, the tone of your voice, the things you say and later regret, your compassion for each other, your support for those you love, and the ways you help each other.

When you feel good about yourself, you can reach out and help others. Helping others should start with your own family. Show interest, love, and concern for them. Compliment and uphold them. Root for them. Offer to help them with their chores.

Chapter 9

People MANNERS AND *Sportsmanship*

manners matter manners matter manners matter manners matter

*U*se good manners out of respect for yourself and others, not because others are courteous, but because you are. Even those who are rude should be treated politely. Don't let a rude person create the atmosphere around you.

Don't encourage rude behavior in others by laughing. Instead, give them a blank look. This clues them in that it was not funny, acceptable, or appropriate. You don't necessarily need to confront the person, but the lack of positive reinforcement will tend to discourage a repeat.

Good manners should always be positive and always prevail. In any confrontation or disagreement a smile is very disarming.

Gracious people show kindness and warmth.

- If you have an overflowing grocery cart, offer to let someone with fewer items get in line ahead of you, especially when stores are busy.

- Say, "May I please," "thank you," and "you're welcome."

- Respond to compliments with, "Thank you."

- Say, "Excuse me?" or "Sir?" or "Ma'am?" when you don't hear what was said.

- Say, "Excuse me" when you walk in front of someone.

- Say, "I'm sorry. Please excuse me," when you bump into someone.

- Offer your chair or seat to an older person who doesn't have one. Let senior citizens go ahead of you whenever possible.

  - Be observant. Offer your chair or seat to anyone who appears fatigued or in greater physical distress than yourself. For example, a pregnant woman or someone using a cane or crutches.

Courteous people show good manners toward others.

- Apologize and ask forgiveness if you hurt someone or make a mistake.

  - Look for the good in people and find it.

  - Open and hold doors for others.

  - Assist others with their coats or packages.

Considerate people are thoughtful and attentive.

- Keep secrets confided in you.

- Don't whisper in front of others, gossip, or tattle.

  - Don't call people names or point out their differences.

  - Befriend unpopular people.

  - Pick up things that don't belong on the floor.

Respectful people admire and appreciate others.

- Children, never contradict your parents or elders in public. (Kids, when parents say, "No," accept it as a positive no. Don't pester them.)

- Show proper respect for your elders and all in authority.

- Husbands and wives should not contradict each other in public.

- Parents, correct children respectfully.

- Give others the same respect you appreciate from them.

- Make everyone in your presence comfortable.

sports AND
recreation ETIQUETTE

Sportsmanship

Fairness, respect for one's opponent, and being a gracious winner or loser is what sportsmanship is all about. Basic rules of conduct apply equally to recreational activities from skydiving to water sports to parlor games and everything in between. Many sports and activities require proper clothing and safety equipment. Respect your fellow sportsmen by following the rules of the game and the dress code.

Parents attending kids' sports events should make it a positive experience for everyone. Going ballistic in response to the referee's or judge's decisions is poor sportsmanship. Remember that you are there to show loving support and encourage your child by rooting for them and their team.

Showing good sportsmanship *teaches* good sportsmanship. Learning to be a good sport builds character, teaches respect for rules and authority, and demonstrates the value of doing your best to achieve goals.

Indoor SPORTS: AT THE *Gym*

Racquet clubs, aerobics classes, fitness, and weight training are some of the activities done at indoor facilities. Consideration for safety and for others will make the experience pleasant for all if you keep these things in mind.

- Wear clean, suitable attire. Immodest clothing is distracting and therefore potentially hazardous to others' safety.

• Joining aerobics classes late distracts others and risks injury to cold muscles.

• Keep personal items where others won't trip over them in both the workout area and the locker room.

• Be considerate of those waiting for machines and equipment. Don't stay to see how the soap opera ends, pause to chat with someone, or make others wait while you rest between sets.

• Use your own towel to wipe perspiration off the equipment so it's ready for the next person.

• If you need music to occupy your mind, bring your own media player and earphones. Keep your wireless phone and other devices silenced.

• If children are welcome at your facility but there is no playroom, bring some type of quiet entertainment such as coloring books—but make sure they don't grind crayons into the floor or mark on anything else.

Outdoor RECREATION

Camping, boating, hiking, beachcombing, and biking are among the many activities where good manners are needed. Exercising caution and courtesy will help prevent accidents and misunderstandings, particularly in crowded recreation areas.

Obey all recreation area rules, place trash in the proper containers, pick up after yourself, collect your belongings, and thank your recreation area host and whoever brought you as their guest.

Never participate in sports under the influence of alcohol or other drugs. Always use the proper safety equipment: bike helmets, life jackets, and so on. They save lives.

Pool PARTIES AND *Beach* TRIPS

- Bring your own towel and plastic bag(s) for your wet, dirty, or sandy towels, clothes, and footwear. And keep those things off of furniture, upholstery, and exterior surfaces of vehicles.

- Obey all pool rules.

- Even excellent swimmers should never swim alone.

Boating

• Boat owners and operators are responsible for the safety of themselves and their passengers. Familiarize passengers (who are old enough) with the boat's controls, and explain to all passengers what to do in an emergency.

• Guests should ask "permission to come aboard" before boarding.

• The boat captain or skipper is in charge. Obey instructions immediately without dispute.

• Always wear the appropriate size and type of PFD (personal flotation device) or life jacket for the waterway and keep it securely buckled at all times.

• Guests should help load and unload the tow vehicle and boat.

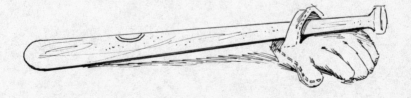

manners matter manners matter manners matter

Guest MANNERS AND *Gratitude*

*W*hen you are invited to someone else's home as a guest, there are a few things you should remember. You need to treat the home with respect and remember that it is their home, not yours.

before YOU leave HOME:

) • Never arrive uninvited without calling ahead to ask if your visit would be welcome or would be more convenient at another time.

• Never bring pets along unless specifically invited to; then monitor your pet closely. Be prepared to apologize, clean up after your pet, and pay for any damage it does. If your pet misbehaves, never bring it with you again.

~ ~ ~

WHEN YOU arrive:

) • Use pathways or sidewalks rather than walking across the yard or through a garden.

• Ask your host where you should park your bike, skateboard, or vehicle while visiting.

• Never leave your vehicle running while you talk to someone at their front door.

guests SHOULD BE courteous:

- Wipe your feet before entering or leave dirty shoes (wet umbrellas, etc.) at the door.

- Hang up your coat properly or put it wherever your host instructs. If your host hangs it up or takes it to another room for you, say "thank you."

- Remove your hat indoors. (Hats, gloves, and so on should stay with your coat.)

- Don't touch ornaments in the home—just look.

- Don't put your feet on the furniture, and don't lean against (or climb) anything—walls, counters, bookshelves, furniture, or vehicles.

- Don't slam doors or run or throw things indoors.

- Clean up after yourself and put things away that you use.

- Never ask for food or refreshments. (You may ask for a glass of water if you're thirsty.) If food or refreshments are offered, remember your manners.

• If you are offered snacks, wash your hands before eating and always put any wrappers in the trash and rinse any dishes and utensils you use.

• Don't try on anyone's clothes or use their perfume or personal care products (such as cosmetics, toothpaste, combs, or hairbrushes).

• Eat at the table, especially if the snacks are messy.

• If hands get sticky, ask where to wash them before touching anything.

• When washing your hands, don't let the dirt end up on the guest towel; get them clean.

RESPECT OTHERS' privacy:

• Don't enter a bedroom, office, den, or other room separated by a doorway without being invited, even if the door is already open.

• Don't open closed doors without knocking. Wait for permission to enter.

153

- Don't look inside the closets, drawers, cupboards, pantry, or refrigerator.

- Don't look through documents or packets of photographs without permission, even if out in plain sight.

  - If you observe someone taking prescription medication, don't ask what it's for. Never ask to use anyone else's allergy prescription (or any prescribed medication).

electronicDEVICES

- Ask permission if you need to use the phone; make sure your host knows whether you're making a local or long distance call, and be brief.

  - Don't turn on the TV, radio, VCR, CD or DVD player, computer, or other electronic device unless invited to. Limit the time you spend using any device alone, such as a single-player computer or video game.

• If you bring your own equipment or entertainment on tape, DVD, CD, or other media to share, always ask permission before connecting anything to your host's equipment.

• Never change the settings or connections on a computer or other electronic device without permission. (If you're allowed to temporarily change a setting, change it back before you're finished or be sure your host knows what to reset after you leave.)

• Don't open computer documents or software programs that may contain private information.

• Never ask your host for the password to access their Internet service. When using their phone line and Internet access, limit the time you spend online.

host MANNERS

- It's impolite to snack on something unless you offer some to your guests.

- When there aren't enough snacks to go around, wait until your guests leave.

- Be sure everyone can join the activities or games. (Don't start a board game for six players when you and your guests total seven.)

- Keep your pets from being overly friendly or assaulting your guests.

- When your guest brings an unwelcome pet or a pet that has misbehaved on previous visits, politely insist your guest keep the pet contained or leashed during the visit.

overnight GUESTS

As an overnight guest, bring along your best behavior and respect the privacy and possessions of your hosts.

Add these rules to your guest manners:

- Know ahead of time exactly how long you're to stay and don't overstay your welcome.

- Don't leave your things all over the house.

- Respect the house curfew and find out what time you should be up to help prepare or be at the table for breakfast.

- Keep the bathroom neat and be quick about your business.

- Fold towels neatly and put them on the towel bars.

- Help clean up and make your bed.

- Thank your hosts for their hospitality when you leave.

~ ~ ~ ~

thank-you NOTES

The logical and polite conclusion to being a guest or receiving a gift is to express your gratitude for your hosts' hospitality and for others' generosity.

Thank-you notes reveal a great deal about your character.

Thank-you notes tell the person who sent the gift that you received it. The sender took the time to select and send the gift; moreover, they thought enough of you to spend time and money on you. The least you can do is say "thank you." Whether you like the gift or not isn't the question.

"Thank you" may be said over the telephone if it's family or something not too significant. A family member living at a distance would probably enjoy hearing your voice. For anyone not as intimate, always write a personal note—never an E-mail except to supplement a mailed thank-you note.

Always mention the gift in your note or whatever kindness you are expressing gratitude for. You don't thank people in order to receive more gifts, but the gifts may stop coming if, in fact, you don't show appreciation.

Send thank-you notes for special dinner parties, luncheons, overnight visits, special favors, and gifts.

Always try to respond within forty-eight hours.

Chapter 11

Community
MANNERS

manners matter manners matter manners matter

*W*e all "belong" to
a community that includes
those on the other side of town
as well as the folks next door.

Community interests affect us all. We use the same roads, stores, library, and police and fire departments, for example. We share the same services. We benefit or suffer together, depending on community conditions.

It's important to apply the Golden Rule in our communities as well as in our homes. Just as healthy bodies need exercise, a healthy community needs citizens who exercise their citizenship. It needs citizens who have eyes to see a need, ears to hear a call for help, feet to rush to help, and hands to fill the need.

Fifty percent of all Americans volunteer on the average of five hours a week. They contribute heavily to the number of Americans who volunteer $150 billion worth of their time each year.

IT'S IMPORTANT TO APPLY

THE *Golden Rule* IN OUR

communities AS WELL AS IN OUR HOMES.

When tragedy strikes, it's clear that we all want to *help* our community rather than *hurt* it. It hurts, for example, when someone litters or commits a crime. It helps when we practice good manners for the good of all and show respect for our environment and our community.

In a sense, life doesn't begin until we get out of the grandstand and get into the game.

Community manners begin in our own neighborhoods. Good neighbors honor the rights, privacy, and property of others. They respect others' religious, political, ethnic, and cultural values.

Being a good neighbor requires minding our own business and not our neighbor's. There are times, however, when our neighbor's business becomes our own if it involves a need we can fill.

If a neighbor is sick and unable to prepare a meal, you can take them one. When neighbors are temporarily unable to perform normal household chores, you can help by feeding their pets, taking out the garbage, picking up the mail and newspaper, or cutting the grass.

Community manners means recognizing needs around us are greater than our own and then serving them. The opportunities to help others are limited only by our willingness to serve. Opportunities include running errands for a shut-in, supplying transportation, visiting nursing homes, reading to the blind, encouraging someone who's "down," and something as simple as sharing a smile and a laugh.

THE BEST EXERCISE FOR *strengthening* THE *heart* IS REACHING DOWN AND *lifting people* UP.

It's nice to see that good community manners live on a two-way street. As citizens show their concern for one another, everyone benefits. Our neighborhood becomes a better place with each act of kindness.

There are several organizations and institutions in our community that can't function without volunteers. They include hospitals, churches, schools, charities of all kinds, service clubs, libraries, Little League, and your local neighborhood watch program.

Each of us has a special talent to offer our hometown and our neighbors. It's good manners to share our abilities.

Be informed about issues and events in your community. Our gardens need attention; so does our community, otherwise weeds will choke out flowers in one and pride of citizenship in the other. Without care, both become jungles, and neighborhoods and property values deteriorate.

Nations that are most enduring are those in which

citizens have the highest sense of civic responsibility and are involved for the common good. If you're eligible, register and exercise your right to vote. Regardless of your age, be involved at the level of your ability. Being involved is a privilege that only freedom allows.

Every community needs *leaders* as well as volunteers. Obviously, we don't become leaders overnight. It takes time, talent, and experience, for example, to become mayor, but every school needs student leaders. Every club needs a president.

church MANNERS

Church is a place for worship and many other wholesome, positive activities.

Going to church should be a worshipful and uplifting experience, and we should go to meet God with the proper attitude. If no one greets you or says "hello," take it upon yourself to greet them with a friendly smile and introduce yourself, ask the person next to you if they are "regulars" or "visiting." This is a way to make friends if you are new or to show hospitality and kindness if they are new. Always try to be friendly—friendliness is part of godliness.

While in church, be attentive, join in the singing, and don't rattle too many candy wrappers or papers. If your children are worshiping with you instead of in the nursery or separate age-appropriate groups, encourage them to be attentive. Don't allow children to use the welcome cards or the day's programs or flyers to express themselves artistically. Instead, come prepared with paper and pencil in case your children need to keep their hands busy. Encourage them to sit quietly, facing forward, with their hands and feet off of the seats and seat backs. If you have decidedly active children, sit near the back so you can discreetly slip out of the service should your restless child become distracting to others.

Couples, save your hugging and stroking for at home. Leaning on or caressing your mate is distracting to those around you.

There are several ways to make church visits more meaningful.

- Attend with a worshipful attitude.

- Remember God ordained the church.

  - Thank God for the freedom to worship.

    - Remember the church belongs to God, not man.

• Apply the sermon to your own life, not your neighbor's.

• Be involved in Sunday school and other rewarding activities.

• Ask the Lord what you can do in your church.

~~~ ~ ~ ~

CHURCH *socials* & *suppers*

This is a good time to remember your manners! Parents should be responsible for the whereabouts of their children. Children should stay with their parents at suppers unless they have permission to leave the hall or the church building.

Sometimes children want to run to the dinner table so they may be free to play with their friends as quickly as possible. Church socials are fun times, but it's necessary for everyone to maintain some order, too.

~~~ ~ ~

THINGS GO *easier* WHEN:

- Children aren't running or pushing to be first in line.

- Children stay with parents unless they have permission to be elsewhere.

- No one is hogging their favorite food.

- No one eats until grace has been said.

- Everyone cleans up after themselves.

- Everyone takes home any dishes they may have brought.

- Everyone shows appreciation to those who helped in the kitchen.

patriot SYMBOLS

Our flag is far more than a colorful piece of cloth. It's a symbol of America's ideals and purpose: an emblem of hope, help, freedom, and opportunity.

When we salute our flag, we're reminded that we are *one nation, under God,* made up of millions of individuals from hundreds of other countries. Our flag flies for all of us.

Because it's such an important symbol, we show special respect for our flag. We allow no other flag to fly above it.

George Washington said of our flag:

WE TAKE THE *stars* AND
blue UNION
FROM *Heaven,*
THE *red* FROM OUR *mother country,*
SEPARATING IT BY
white STRIPES, THUS SHOWING
WE HAVE SEPARATED FROM HER,
AND THE WHITE STRIPES SHALL GO
DOWN TO
POSTERITY REPRESENTING
liberty.

Our flag is really a symbol of ourselves. It is what we make it. We inherit it with proud, flying colors. For over two hundred years, our people raised it to the highest symbol of freedom and justice in all history. Our dreams, our faith, our allegiance keep it flying.

Every time we perform an act of kindness for a neighbor, each time we render service to our community, we not only knit the fabric of our society a little tighter, we also strengthen the bond of the stars and stripes. Our flag will fly in peace and freedom as long as we pull *together* and not pull *apart*.

Today, community is no longer measured by fences, county lines, or even oceans. Space shuttles and satellites remind us that the earth has become the ultimate community. What happens next door and on the next block not only affects us; what happens on the next continent can also affect us. As a result, we don't want to keep our good manners at home. They need to cross oceans and touch every corner of our world.

The *opportunities* to help others are limited only by our *willingness* to *serve*.

Chapter 12

Travel MANNERS

manners matter manners matter manners

Road rage is an outrage and can be life-threatening. Thoughtless individuals make remarks that delay departure times in airports, train stations, or bus depots. People leave threatening notes or abandon items that force the transportation industry to take drastic precautions. Transportation hubs can be shut down for hours while security checks are conducted. Pilots are forced to make unscheduled stops to have belligerent, out-of-control passengers arrested. Dozens or hundreds of passengers' lives are disrupted, and travel-related fears escalate.

EXERCISING EXTRA *courtesy* AND *caution* WILL HELP SMOOTH THE WAY NO MATTER HOW YOU TRAVEL.

automobiles

When you're driving, treat your passengers as guests by making them feel welcome and comfortable. You are responsible for the safety of others, so insist on reasonable behavior for passengers of all ages. It's impossible to concentrate on the road if someone is distracting you or screaming in the backseat.

When you're the guest, be courteous and minimize distractions. Show your appreciation for the driver's kindness and hospitality.

BASIC driving MANNERS

- Fasten seat belts. Lock the doors. Keep seat belts fastened until you exit the car.

- Never drive or ride with someone when there are more people than seat belts.

- Sit where the driver says to, without complaint.

- Keep music and other noises low so the driver can hear what's going on with their vehicle, traffic, or sirens.

- Keep hands, feet, and other things to yourself and inside the car.

- Keep feet on the floor, not on seats or seat backs, and don't smudge windows.

• Don't eat or drink in the car unless the driver invites you to.

• Don't smoke. The space is too confined for good air quality and clear thinking.

• Keep conversation light and pleasant; never argue when driving.

• Choose music that won't irritate others.

• Don't startle the driver by shouting because you saw something interesting.

• Don't be a backseat driver.

• Let one another know if you're too warm or too cold, need a rest room break, or are getting hungry or thirsty.

• Men should open a car door for women and children when entering or exiting a vehicle (especially in dark or secluded locations).

• Adults and teenagers should open car doors for young children.

- Make sure it's safe before opening the car door to let others out.

- Passengers should enter and exit a vehicle on the curb or sidewalk side of the vehicle.

- Parking spaces can be narrow: Don't bump another vehicle with your door, bags, packages, grocery cart, stroller, backpack, or yourself.

- Check the backseat for hidden intruders before unlocking a parked vehicle.

guestsONlongDRIVES

- Start your trip freshly showered and in clean clothes.

- Use the rest room before you leave.

- Pack light for trips and ask ahead of time how much luggage, money, types of clothing, and which personal items you should bring.

• Ask if you can bring snacks to share. Don't bring messy snacks.

• Ask before you leave when you'll be stopping for meals or for breaks. Eat breakfast at home if the first planned stop is for lunch.

• If you tend to get carsick, forewarn the driver. Alert them immediately if you feel carsick.

• Children should wait for adults to open car doors.

kids, WHEN YOU enter THE CAR:

• Greet everyone with a big smile.

• Say hello, using their names.

• Fasten your seat belt.

• Remain cheerful and cooperative.

• Remember to show your appreciation.

- Look for ways to make the ride more pleasant:

  - Enjoy a good conversation.

  - Observe the scenery.

  - Play fun word games (quietly).

  - Keep your noises and voice level low.

  - Stop immediately if you are asked to stop doing something.

WHEN YOU return

- Thank the driver and the person who invited you.

- Make sure you have all your belongings.

- Say a pleasant "good-bye" to everyone in the car.

never RIDE WITH strangers!

Do not, under any circumstances, accept a ride from a stranger, no matter how nice they seem.

~~~~~

air TRAVEL: WAIT, AND wait SOME MORE

Think ahead. Impeccable pretrip grooming is always appreciated. Strong scents in close quarters, whether it's food or cologne, can worsen motion sickness—which could increase odor problems exponentially. People traveling with children should be well prepared for a long, tedious trip with plenty of quiet things to do.

Watch what you say. Never make comments or jokes that could be misinterpreted. Stay calm when flights or other conveyances are overbooked or delayed or luggage is temporarily lost.

Keep bags and carry-on items in sight *at all times*.

Disregard one courtesy: Never agree to watch or carry a stranger's luggage—it could contain illegal substances or explosives—leaving you "holding the bag."

Strive to be quick, efficient, and polite when loading and unloading at the curb and dealing with skycaps, ticket agents, passengers, and security personnel.

Wait patiently in ticket counter lines, at security gates, and when preparing to board. Apologize sincerely if you bump into someone.

As you board, move carefully but promptly to your seat and load overhead compartments quickly. Don't block the aisle to fastidiously arrange your things. The last person to stow items should latch the compartment securely, but assist others whenever you're better situated or they need help.

Nod or say hello to your seatmate and sit down. If someone is reading, writing, or otherwise absorbed in something, they would prefer not to be disturbed or engage in conversation. Exchanging pleasantries and conversing is fine. But when they pick up something to do or ask for a headset, they're ready to stop chatting.

Be considerate about reading lights, headset or conversation volume, and tray and seat back positions. Keep your things and yourself within your allotted space.

Window seat passengers should look around and consider others' wishes before adjusting shades.

Keep rest room visits brief, flush and leave things clean, touch as few surfaces as possible, and wash your hands well before you exit.

Well before the flight lands, stow your personal items and follow the flight crew's instructions.

Remove overhead articles carefully. A cascade of heavy items might ruin someone's day.

Chapter 13

Tips AND Gratuities

*T*ipping is a longstanding custom that rewards another for their service. Whether at home or away, good manners require tipping appropriately.

 **HANDLERS:**

- Skycaps and Porters: $1 to $1.50 per bag, $2 each for weighty bags.

Hotels:

- Bellhop: For bringing bags to your room, $1 to $1.50 per bag, $2 each for weighty bags. For bringing other items after you've checked in, tip $2; for special errands, tip $5.

- Maid: $2 to $3 per night.

- Concierge: $5 per day that he or she does something for you.

- Parking valet: $2 for bringing your car to you.

- Doorman: $1 for hailing a cab ($2 in harsh weather).

- Room service: 15 percent (if not already added to the bill).

Dining:

• Waiters: 15 to 20 percent of the bill, 10 percent for poor service, blatantly rude treatment deserves no tip.

• Bartenders: 10 to 15 percent of the tab.

• Cocktail waiters: 15 percent of the tab.

• Wine stewards and sommeliers: 10 to 15 percent of the wine cost (in addition to the meal cost including the wine cost).

• Lunch counters and buffets: 10 percent.

• Carhops: 10 percent.

• Take-out delivery: $1 to $2 depending on order size and weather conditions.

WHETHER AT HOME OR AWAY, GOOD *manners* REQUIRE *tipping* APPROPRIATELY.

Attendants:

- Rest room attendants: 25 to 50 cents for hand-ing you a towel, the standard service. Add $1 for assistance removing a stain or providing cologne, hairspray, or hand lotion.

- Cloakroom attendants: Tip $1 per coat checked.

- Parking lot attendants: $1 for basic service.

Personal SERVICES:

- Hairstylists: 15 to 20 percent for a haircut, color, or perm. For having your hair set or washed and blow-dried, tip 15 percent.

- Manicurists: either $2 or 15 percent of the cost.

HIRED *Drivers:*

- Taxi drivers: 15 percent, 50 cents as a minimum, and for very short rides round up to the next dollar. Tip extra if you're stuck in traffic jams and omit the tip if the driver took the longest possible route and ran up the fare.

- Limousines: 15 to 20 percent of the bill.

- Tour bus drivers: $2 to $4 per day; Tour guides: $3 to $5 per day.

Chapter 14

THE *Business* COMMUNITY: *Manners* AT *Work*

*I*n the business world, manners matter perhaps more than in any other sphere of activity. Certain behavior is to be desired and affects everything from pleasing customers and keeping their business to pleasing the boss and keeping one's job.

BUSINESS etiquette

Business etiquette is a priority in the workplace. Good manners in the way you present yourself will offer a competitive edge. Your behavior sets the tone and says who you really are. It conveys a confidence whereby you are comfortable at any level. Good manners make for good business.

Business etiquette means behaving in an acceptable and refined way. The Golden Rule applies here as much if not more than anywhere else if you have any desire to climb the corporate ladder.

~~~

meetings

When you schedule a meeting or interview, do your best to allow everyone enough time to prepare and be sure to check on the availability of everyone you want to attend *before* you schedule it. Punctuality is always important at meetings. Don't bring food or drinks to a meeting unless you are told in advance that it's okay. Silence your wireless phone, pager, watch, and other devices.

interviews

Take your manners with you on a business interview, and let it begin with an appropriate, polished, respectable-looking resumé.

- Be no more than five minutes early.

- Bring an extra copy of your resumé and a typed list of references (be sure they know to expect calls about your job skills or character).

- Wear clean, well-pressed clothes appropriate for the job.

- Arrive well groomed from head to toe.

- Everything about you will be noticed.

Thank the interviewer for the meeting with you, show interest, and be alert. Be deliberate in your answers, smile, make eye contact, and display the qualities of diplomacy and respect that would exemplify a top-notch employee.

Send a thank-you letter immediately, recapping your interview, and express your interest in the job.

manners ON THE job

How you behave at work is a reflection of you, your work, and your company as a whole. Think about that before you take off your shoes or put your feet up on your desk. Your work space is also a reflection of you and your work. Whether you have a desk, office, cubicle, or some other workstation, keep it neat. Don't overdecorate your work space. Tasteful and tidy is the key.

Use conduct and language appropriate for a work environment, but don't stoop to the lowest level in order to fit in with peers. Know what your company's policy is regarding behavior that may be considered inappropriate. As a rule, profanity isn't appreciated by a majority of coworkers.

Being overly familiar with coworkers, making suggestive comments, or touching someone because of their gender generally amounts to uninvited and unwelcome conduct—which can lead to serious legal trouble for the individual *and* their employer. Avoid gestures, comments, and facial expressions that may be interpreted or considered as outright profanity, discrimination, or sexual harassment.

BEING considerate

Conflicts inevitably arise in the office or workplace. When they do, begin by discussing the issue privately, calmly, and politely with the person—no one else. If you cannot resolve the conflict, suggest that you ask someone at the next level of authority to help resolve it. Let them know that you feel it's important to get it settled properly, even if it turns out you were both mistaken. Your willingness to resolve a conflict shows your respect for your coworkers and your company's policies. Once a conflict is resolved, it's wise to go back and smooth things over with your coworker. Never underestimate the value of maintaining good working relationships.

Think how necessary it is before disturbing someone in a cubicle or office. Knock before entering and make it short.

While it can be tempting to gossip, keep the Golden Rule in mind. Never talk about anyone else's private business without their permission, or if they are not present. It isn't fair, and it makes others wonder what kinds of things you reveal about *them* in *their* absence.

BUSINESS telephone
ETIQUETTE

Leave a personalized greeting on your voice mail. If you will be in meetings or unavailable for much of the day, change your voice mail message so callers know what to expect. If possible, state when you plan to return calls and return voice mail messages promptly. Let callers know who can help them in your absence or in the case of an emergency. If you have children in day care or a seriously ill relative, let your caregivers or close family members know who to call in the case of a family emergency.

WHEN YOU leave SOMEONE A voice MAIL:

• Identify yourself with your first and last name (spelling it may be appropriate for first-time callers).

• Give your company name when appropriate.

• Give the day and time you're calling. (Most

voice mail systems record the day and time of incoming calls, but no system is infallible.)

• State the reason for your call.

• Give your phone number carefully (so the person can write it down without having to replay your message) and say, "Again, that number is. . ." (Their Caller ID may record where your call came from, but that may not be where you can be reached later.)

• Indicate if you want a return call and the best time to reach you.

• End the call with "thank you" and "good-bye."

rude BUSINESS
telephone BEHAVIOR

• Keeping inefficient or out-dated communications equipment.

• Abrupt, apathetic, and garbled greetings.

• Not identifying yourself by first and last name when you answer or call.

• Demanding to speak with someone.

• Long delays before answering the phone or connecting callers to voice mail.

• Too many automated options with no way out.

• Keeping callers on long holds. (Check back every thirty seconds to see if the caller still wants to hold, leave a message or a voice mail, or have you call them back.)

• Forgotten holds. (Anyone on hold longer than thirty seconds will think you forgot about them.)

• Interrupting the caller to transfer them, presumably to "someone who cares."

• Telling a busy switch-board operator your life story. (Save the details for the appropri-ate person.)

• No voice mail or a full voice mailbox.

- Unreturned phone calls.

- Faxing ads or long documents without permission.

- Faxing pages with large, blacked-out areas.

- Fax machines repeatedly dialing the wrong number.

customer INTERACTIONS

Whether you are the buyer or the salesperson, on the phone or dealing with people in person, rudeness and abruptness get you nowhere. The Golden Rule works just as well here: Treat salespeople and customers with the courtesy and respect you want from them.

- Treat every customer as if they are your best customer and make them feel that meeting their need is your top priority.

- Be as kind to your employees and coworkers as you are to your best customers.

- Be pleasant but persistent. Don't be demanding.

- Do your best to meet delivery commitments, order completions, refunds or credits, and replacements promptly.

- Respond to phone calls, E-mails, faxes, and letters promptly.

- Acknowledge orders with appreciation and provide estimated delivery dates, then notify clients when orders have been shipped.

- Take the opportunity to thank them again for their order.

- If a customer's order will be delayed, apologize and explain why and when they can expect the order. Thank them for their patience and understanding.

- If you simply cannot fulfill an order, help the customer get it from another source. They'll remember that your top priority was helping them, not your bottom line, and will want to do business with you again someday.

internet AND e-mail MANNERS

Your company may present a professional image and have lots of polished marketing materials, but if your E-mail content is sloppy or unprofessional it will undermine customers' confidence in you and your business.

WRITING e-mail

- E-mail is written communication: Use standard writing guidelines, proper grammar and punctuation, as well as professional language.

- Never SHOUT by typing in all caps, be casual but use a polite, respectful tone. Never correct the spelling, grammar, or punctuation of others.

- Be specific in your subject line.

- If your business E-mail address does not identify you by name or your company's name, include your first and last name in your message as well as your company name.

• Use a salutation such as "Dear Mr. James," or "Good morning, Mike," and end with a complimentary closing such as "Sincerely, Tim Thumb" or "Yours truly, Sarah Sprat." Include your phone number or indicate the best way or time to reach you.

• Compose E-mail with a tactful, service-oriented approach. Be clear and to the point and respond to every E-mail promptly. E-mail between coworkers should always be courteous and professional. An unprofessional E-mail inadvertently sent to the wrong person will do permanent damage to the relationship.

• Be sure that your E-mail or online postings contain nothing that you would be embarrassed to see in the news-paper or hear on the nightly news.

GOOD *manners* MAKE FOR
good BUSINESS.

forwarding E-MAIL

- The average person gets twenty or more E-mails a day. Don't forward jokes, chain letters, and so on unless you are sure the recipient wants you to.

- Use caution when forwarding files and E-mail. Use good, up-to-date virus protection software to prevent spreading viruses. Notify people in your address book immediately if your computer becomes infected with a virus.

- Delete the E-mail addresses and messages to previous recipients before you forward E-mail. Use the "BC" or blind copy option to protect others' privacy.

• When you reply to an E-mail, copy the relevant part of their message into your reply. Don't send blunt, single-word responses.

• Never give out someone's private E-mail address without permission and get permission before sending links to web sites.

• Never add E-mail addresses you acquire online to your advertising list (or anyone else's list) without their permission.

INSTANT messaging

• Instant messaging is convenient and fun, and possibly intrusive. When you begin an instant message, always ask if it is a good time for an E-chat.

• Employers will appreciate your E-chatting just as much as your making personal calls when you should be working.

kitchens AND
lunchrooms

Most businesses have a kitchen or lunchroom for employee use. Treat them with respect by cleaning up after yourself, making a fresh pot of coffee if you take the last cup (or rinsing and turning off the coffeemaker), alerting the purchasing clerk or ordering supplies when they run low, and removing your leftovers from the refrigerator before they become science projects.

epilogue

Manners Matter—Living the Golden Rule for Kids of All Ages doesn't presume to be the final word on the subject. . . only a guide. We hope you find it interesting and helpful in your home.

These chapters don't cover every aspect of etiquette because we've tried to stick to basics. We've concentrated on the life experiences we're most likely to encounter, to emphasize those things that go to the heart of the matter: courtesy, attitude, behavior, relationships, and love. *The best way to measure manners is to use the Golden Rule.* The manners that matter most touch more than our style; they touch our lives.

the author

Hermine Hartley is described by her husband as a Proverbs 31 wife and has earned degrees in motherhood, grandmotherhood, and happy homemaking. She and her husband, Al, have two children and six grandchildren. The Hartleys make their home in Florida.